B 374348

TWO REPORTS ON THE REORGANIZATION & RECONSTRUCTION OF THE NEW YORK CITY PRISON SYSTEM

By

HASTINGS H. HART
Consultant on Correctional Institutions for the
Regional Plan of New York

I. SUPPLEMENTARY REPORT
PRESENTED JANUARY 7, 1925

II. ORIGINAL REPORT
PRESENTED NOVEMBER 20, 1924

PUBLISHED BY
THE PRISON ASSOCIATION OF NEW YORK
135 EAST 15TH STREET
NEW YORK CITY

MARCH, 1925

TWO REPORTS ON THE REORGANIZATION & RECONSTRUCTION OF THE NEW YORK CITY PRISON SYSTEM

By
HASTINGS H. HART
Consultant on Correctional Institutions for the
Regional Plan of New York

I. SUPPLEMENTARY REPORT
PRESENTED JANUARY 7, 1925

II. ORIGINAL REPORT
PRESENTED NOVEMBER 20, 1924

PUBLISHED BY
THE PRISON ASSOCIATION OF NEW YORK
135 EAST 15TH STREET
NEW YORK CITY

MARCH, 1925

Prison Assoc. of N.Y.
4-18-1925

HV
9481
.N5
H32

LETTER OF HON. GEORGE W. WICKERSHAM

40 Wall Street, New York
January 21, 1924

Dr. Hastings H. Hart,
Ex-President American Prison Association,
130 East 22d Street, New York, N. Y.

Dear Dr. Hart:

A group of which I am acting as chairman would like to support recommendations (in so far as they are sound) which have been made by the Commissioner of Correction to the Board of Estimate and Apportionment, for an adequate reorganization and reconstruction on modern lines and in suitable localities of the penal and correctional institutions of this city. In order to do so effectively we need to have an up-to-date examination and report of the actual conditions of each of these various institutions, not from the point of view of administration, but from the point of view of construction, equipment and location, including questions of fire hazards, sanitation, possibility of economic and suitable occupation, including outdoor work and exercise, and suitability of the buildings from point of view of effective prison discipline.

Your long experience in charitable and correctional work, and your recent experience as President of the American Prison Association, and in surveys of prisons in the City of St. Louis and the State of Pennsylvania, and other localities, fit you to a very exceptional degree to prepare such a report. If you can arrange to do so, the group, of which I speak above, would like you to undertake this service in its behalf. We would undertake to secure for you the necessary permits from the Department of Correction.

I am,

Very sincerely yours,
GEORGE W. WICKERSHAM,
Chairman.

PREFACE

The two reports submitted herewith were prepared at the request of Hon. George W. Wickersham, representing a group of organizations interested in improving the prison system of the City of New York.

A report was submitted on November 24th. After the preparation of this report, the situation with reference to the prison program of the Commissioner of Correction for the City of New York changed, and at the request of Mr. Wickersham a supplementary report was prepared and submitted January 7, 1925.

These two reports are printed in the following pamphlet.

The supplementary report is printed first because it presents the subject in condensed form and brings it down to date. The report of November 24, 1924, which is printed second, treats of the New York prison situation more in detail and indicates the reasons for the recommendations contained in the supplementary report.

This report is intended to harmonize with and to emphasize the admirable report of the August Grand Jury, published in December, 1924. I have, however, gone farther than the Grand Jury report in recommending what appears to me to be the logical outcome of that report, namely, that Riker's Island should not only furnish the site for the new penitentiary, but that the distribution work tentatively established some time ago at the penitentiary be established and properly developed in a distinct institution on Riker's Island. I am recommending also that drug addicts shall continue to be kept on the Island, but that a separate prison in its own enclosure shall be provided for the treatment and industrial employment of drug addicts after they have received hospital treatment elsewhere. This plan would reduce the number of drug addicts kept on Riker's Island.

I have indicated also why it appears to be necessary to revise the plans for the new penitentiary which were prepared seventeen years ago.

It appears to be extremely important that the entire plan for the future use of Riker's Island should be considered before any permanent building operations are undertaken on the Island.

HASTINGS H. HART.

NEW YORK, March 2, 1925

TABLE OF CONTENTS

	PAGE
LETTER OF HON. GEORGE W. WICKERSHAM	3
PREFACE	5

SUPPLEMENTARY REPORT OF JANUARY, 1925

RECOMMENDATIONS OF GRAND JURY ENDORSED

1. Abandonment of Welfare Island for Prisons... 12
2. Unfitness of Welfare Island for Drug Addicts... 12
3. Transfer of Penitentiary and Correction Hospital... 12
4. Riker's Island as Site for New Penitentiary... 12
5. Use of Prison Labor in Construction Work... 13
6. Use of Prisoners for Handling Waste Material... 13

ADDITIONAL RECOMMENDATIONS BY THE WRITER

1. A Separate Distributing Prison... 13
2. The New Penitentiary (as above)... 13
3. A Separate Custodial Department for Drug Addicts... 13
4. Removal of Hospital for Drug Addicts from Riker's Island... 14
5. Discontinue Commitment of Felons... 15
6. Prohibition of Doubling-up in Cells... 16
7. Revision of Plans for New Penitentiary... 16

A GREAT OPPORTUNITY AT RIKER'S ISLAND... 19

ORIGINAL REPORT OF NOVEMBER, 1924

PRISONS ON WELFARE ISLAND... 23
   The New York County Penitentiary... 24
      Employment of Prisoners... 24
      Introduction of Contraband Material... 25
      The Penitentiary as a Clearing House... 25

A NEW DISTRIBUTING PRISON... 26
   The Correction Hospital... 27
   The Women's Farm Colony at Greycourt... 27

PRISONS ON WELFARE ISLAND SHOULD BE REMOVED... 28

HART'S ISLAND—THE BRANCH PENITENTIARY... 29
   The Potter's Field... 30
   Present Area of Hart's Island... 31

FUTURE LOCATION OF THE PENITENTIARY... 32
   Putnam County, Orange County, or Long Island... 33
   Riker's Island, the Best Proposed Site... 34
      Value of Riker's Island... 35
      Made Ground... 35
      Present Use of Riker's Island... 36
      Future Uses of Riker's Island... 37

	PAGE
Should Not Be Used Exclusively for Drug Addicts	37
For Penitentiary	37
For New Distributing Prison	38
Recommendations Respecting Riker's Island	39
Distributing Prison	39
Constructive Prison Labor	39
INDUSTRIAL ORGANIZATION	40
FUTURE POPULATION OF CITY CORRECTIONAL INSTITUTIONS	42
Table I—Prisoners Received	42
Diagram A	43
Table II—Average Number of Prisoners	44
Diagram B	45
Table III—Total Number in Custody	46
Table IV—Population Compared with Capacity	47
TREATMENT OF DRUG ADDICTS	48
An Irrational System	48
A Rational Plan	49
A New Hospital for Drug Addicts	50
A Reformatory for Drug Addicts	50
Table V—Commitments of Drug Addicts	51
Table VI—Drug Addicts at Riker's Island	52
CONCLUSION	52

PART I
SUPPLEMENTARY REPORT OF JANUARY 7, 1925

A SUPPLEMENTARY REPORT ON THE REORGANIZATION AND RECONSTRUCTION OF THE NEW YORK CITY PRISON SYSTEM

New York, January 7, 1925.

HON. GEORGE W. WICKERSHAM,
40 Wall Street,
New York City.

Dear Sir:

On January 21, 1924, representing a group of organizations interested in improving the prison system of the City of New York, you requested me to make "an up-to-date examination and report of the actual conditions of each of" the institutions under the control of the Commissioner of Correction, with special reference to "the removal of the penal institutions from Welfare Island" and "an adequate reorganization and reconstruction on modern lines and in suitable localities of the penal and correctional institutions of the city." You stated that the group which you represented "would like to support recommendations (in so far as they were sound) which have been made by the Commissioner of Correction to the Board of Estimate and Apportionment." This request also involved consideration of the branch penitentiary on Hart's Island and the Women's Farm Colony at Greycourt, New York, which institutions are closely related to the penitentiary.

Acting on this request, I submitted to you a preliminary report on June 24, 1924, and a revision of that report on November 20, 1924.

Since the filing of my original and revised reports the Grand Jury of New York County, August Term, has filed its report on the same subject, accompanied by a report of a special committee of the regular grand jury. This report is accompanied by communications from the Hon. Frederick A. Wallis, Commissioner of Correction, and the Hon. Bird S. Coler, Commissioner of Welfare, which, together with the report of the grand jury and its special committee, make a material change in the situation relative to the proposed removal and reconstruction of the penitentiary.[1]

I am in receipt of your letter of December 24, in which you say: "Some of the members of our committee ask if you could prepare a supplementary report or conclusion to that which you have already made for us, taking into consideration this change in plan and pointing out the advantages of completing the building of the new penitentiary at Riker's Island at the earliest possible time."

Acting upon this new request, I beg leave to submit for your consideration the following supplementary report and recommendations, in the light of the documents above mentioned.

The report of the grand jury and the accompanying report of its special committee are unique documents in the annals of grand juries and ought to be read by every intelligent citizen of Greater New York. They carry an impression of intelligent study, comprehension, progress, practical humanity and common sense, which are rarely seen in grand jury reports. The special committee has manifestly given a large amount of patient and intelligent study to the complex and difficult questions involved, and their conclusions are entitled to the patient and considerate attention of their constituents, since they propose rational and economical solutions of difficulties with which the city has struggled vainly for more than half a century.

A. Recommendations Endorsed

I heartily endorse the findings and recommendations of the Grand Jury and its special committee on the following points:

1. The abandonment of Welfare Island as a location for prisons.[2]
2. The unfitness of Welfare Island as a site for a hospital for drug addicts.[3]
3. The transfer of the Penitentiary and the Correction Hospital to some other locations.[4]
4. The acceptance of Riker's Island as the only readily available and practical site for the new penitentiary.[5]

[1] For fuller information, see pp. 28, 29.   [2] For fuller information, see pp. 24, 27.
[3] For fuller information, see pp. 25, 27.   [4] For fuller information, see pp. 36, 37.
[5] For fuller information, see pp. 32–34, 37.

5. The use of prison labor in the construction of the new penitentiary.[1]
6. The use of prisoners instead of free laborers for unloading scows and léveling waste material in Riker's Island, and for salvaging useful material therefrom.[2]

I believe that these six recommendations will command the assent of every intelligent student of the New York City prison situation.

B. ADDITIONAL RECOMMENDATIONS

I recommend that three institutions be located and built on Riker's Island—each to form a separate and distinct department, but to be administered by the Commissioner of Correction, with a competent superintendent for each department and with common purchasing department, warehouse, heating and power plant, laundry and bakery: namely, a distributing prison, a new penitentiary and a separate prison for drug addicts.

1. **A separate distributing prison** with clinics and laboratories. The Legislature of 1916 enacted a law providing that the penitentiary should be a classification prison. Effort has been made to carry out this law, but the attempt to do this work in the penitentiary has been unsuccessful because of the unavoidable conditions in that institution. The distributing prison should have an immediate capacity of 300 to 350, and later on a capacity of 400 to 500. This department should not provide permanent care for any prisoners, but, after making necessary case studies and clinical observations and having given the prisoner such medical, surgical, dental or psychiatric treatment as he may require, should then transfer them promptly to that institution which is best adapted to meet the needs of the individual.[3]

2. **The new penitentiary, as above recommended,** with a capacity of 600 to 800 prisoners. The Branch Penitentiary on Hart's Island also can continue to receive prisoners from the new distributing prison on Riker's Island on a classified basis.[4]

3. **A separate and distinct custodial department** for the confinement of male drug addicts after receiving hospital treatment

---

[1] For fuller information, see pp. 37–39.
[2] For fuller information, see pp. 39–41.
[3] For fuller information, see pp. 25–26, 38–39.
[4] For fuller information, see pp. 29–32.

of from four to six weeks. This department should be secluded by an 18-foot wall similar to the wall which surrounds the New Jersey State Reformatory at Rahway, New Jersey, or a 10-foot double barbed wire fence, in order to guard against the surreptitious introduction of drugs and other contraband material. There should be room for five or six acres of truck gardening for outdoor employment, and shops should be provided for industrial employment and vocational training. This department should be the normal development of the hospital for drug addicts now on the island.[1]

The following changes in practice in the treatment of drug addicts should be made:

(a) No "voluntary commitments" should be made to the custodial institution. All inmates should be committed by the courts on equal terms. Voluntary cases should be dealt with separately from committed cases and the present practice of prohibiting a second volunteer entry should continue.[2]

(b) All inmates should be committed on an indefinite sentence and a thoroughly efficient parole system should be adopted, with high-grade parole officers.[3]

(c) The law should be so amended as to provide cumulative sentences. The first commitment might be made for a maximum of six months; the second for a maximum of a year; the third for a maximum of two years; the fourth for a maximum of three years.

Under the present system a large part of the drug addicts are sent on flat sentences of 100 days, at the end of which they are discharged without supervision and usually without money, and sometimes wearing summer clothes in winter. The only friend of the discharged addict is the drug vender, who gives him employment selling drugs or favors him with a gratuitous "shot," and his condition is very soon as bad as ever.

Some drug addicts have been committed to Riker's Island from twelve to fifteen times each. It costs the city $3.00 a day per inmate for maintenance. After fifteen commitments the city will have spent $4,500 in a course of treatment which was bound to fail from the start.

4. The Removal of the Hospital for Male Drug Addicts from Riker's Island.—This hospital should be located in the Borough

[1] For fuller information, see pp. 15, 37, 50. [2] For fuller information, see pp. 15, 49
[4] For fuller information, see p. 50.

of Manhattan, or Brooklyn, possibly in connection with Bellevue Hospital. It should be placed in the upper stories of a cruciform hospital building on the general plan of the Fifth Avenue Hospital, and the arrangement should be such as to guard absolutely against the surreptitious introduction of drugs.

A roof garden should give opportunity for outdoor air and exercise, and medical work should be carried on by a staff of expert physicians in order to secure the scientific treatment of the habit.

On completion of the course of hospital treatment patients should be promptly transferred to the custodial department on Riker's Island, where they should be placed under an efficient reformatory discipline and should work according to their strength and ability at productive employment organized on the occupational therapy plan, which has had such marked success in the Indiana Hospital for Insane Criminals at Michigan City and in the insane hospitals of the State of Massachusetts.

No "self-committed" patients should be sent to Riker's Island. Heretofore many persons with known criminal records have been accepted as "self-committed" patients. Such individuals should receive court commitment and should serve time at Riker's Island after completing their preliminary hospital treatment.

Under the proposed system there would be some reasonable prospect of curing a portion of the men committed for treatment, and those who proved incorrigible would be detained for periods of increasing length and would be made to earn their living instead of being a constant menace both to themselves and to the community.

5. The discontinuance of the commitment of felons under workhouse and penitentiary sentences to the New York County Penitentiary and securing legislation for the commitment of all such felons to state prisons.

The penitentiary problem will be much simplified if the institution be used exclusively for misdemeanant prisoners, and if the felons who are now committed to the penitentiary be sent to state prisons. The presence of long term felons who are likely to endeavor to escape will necessitate an unnecessary expense for strong construction to retain such prisoners. Prisoners committed for short terms and for minor offenses are much less likely to attempt to escape, and the escape of such prisoners is a matter of minor importance. Prisoners of this class are being safely kept in simple buildings of greatly reduced cost in many institutions: for example, the Indiana State Farm for misdemeanant prisoners and the Workhouse of the District of Columbia at Occoquan.

6. Prohibition of "Doubling-up."—The confinement of two prisoners in one cell should be absolutely prohibited in all prisons of the city of New York. If at any time it becomes necessary to confine more than one prisoner in a room, the dormitory principle should be adopted, with not less than three prisoners in one room—never two.

The practice of locking up two prisoners in a cell directly promotes the worst vices of which the human race is capable, and results in the corruption of many young prisoners who have not previously indulged in such practices.

7. Revision of Plans for the New Penitentiary.—The report of the Grand Jury refers to the fact that in 1908 plans were made for a new penitentiary and the architects were paid $76,500 for their work on the plans which are now the property of the Department of Correction. The Grand Jury says of these plans: "They are in excellent condition and we were assured that with slight alteration they would be acceptable for present use. It would seem to be most desirable to utilize these plans, which were the result of so eminent a competition and subsequent study and revision by competent experts for several years and are now, after the expenditure of a large sum of money on them, the property of the city."[1]

The special committee of the Grand Jury wisely remarks respecting these plans: "It must be borne in mind that in 1908 a competition was held of some of the best architects in the city, and that the plans which were finally accepted and paid for by the city were the best available at that time. In the last twenty-five years, to the best of our knowledge, the important changes in prison architecture which have been adopted, the worth of which has been proved beyond the experimental stage, are: less monumental and more economical construction; the sanitary features, including toilets and wash-bowls in the individual cells, the outside cell construction, which provides better light and ventilation, and the abolishment of the dark or punishment cells."[2]

---

[1] A Study . . . by a Special Committee of the Regular Grand Jury, August Term, 1924, p. 14.

[2] *Ibid.*, p. 41.

It is very desirable to utilize the expensive plans already made as far as practicable, but unquestionably revision of these plans will be unavoidable, as is clearly recognized in the paragraph of the report of the special committee above quoted, and the Commissioner of Correction should have authority to make necessary changes.

If the suggestions which I have made should be adopted, making three separate departments on Riker's Island, the distribution prison, the penitentiary, and the custodial institution for drug addicts, it will be necessary to have three buildings for the housing of prisoners instead of one, as contemplated by the original plans.

This change will diminish rather than increase the cost of the plant, because the cell house or dormitories for the drug addicts can be of much simpler construction than the elaborate cell house contemplated in the plans.

It will be necessary to provide a suitable cell house with individual cells for the distribution prison, and it would be necessary to provide single cells for perhaps one-third of the penitentiary population, but much simpler and inexpensive buildings will serve for the drug addicts, as is shown by the fact that they are now safely kept in flimsy wooden dormitories and, as the grand jury points out, one strong building on the Island has been disused.

During the past fifteen years, and especially during the past ten years, there has come about a marked change in the ideas of prison managers and architects with reference to prison construction. As the committee has stated, this tendency is in favor of less monumental and more economical construction and also of the use of outside cells, like those in the new Sing Sing prison and the Westchester County Penitentiary.

This change has arisen from two causes: First, the recognition of the fact that strong tool-proof cells are needed for only a fraction of the prisoners of the misdemeanant class. The majority of these prisoners are not jail breakers and are not disposed to vigorous efforts for escape, and competent prison officers can readily discover which prisoners need to be rigorously confined. The second cause for the modification of prison plans is economy. Since the war the cost of prison construction has practically doubled from what it was fifteen years ago. The state of Ohio is erecting an administration building for a prison intended for 3,000 men, and the lowest bid for building the prison was $14,000,000. It has been found necessary to modify the plans. The state of Pennsylvania is building a new prison for 3,000 men near Bellefonte, in the center of the state, and it is estimated that the construction of that prison on its original designs would have cost $18,000,000 to $20,000,000. The prison board scrapped plans which cost $36,000 and are now modifying seriously a second set of expensive plans in the interests of economy.

The city of Detroit is building a new House of Correction for which elaborate plans were made. After the construction was begun these plans were radically modified in order to reduce the cost. The District of Columbia is now building a reformatory for young men at Lorton, Virginia. Congress made very limited appropriations for this work, and the managers of the prison were compelled to devise more economical building plans. This has been done with remarkable success and they are now constructing a reformatory designed for 800 prisoners which is estimated to cost less than $1,000 per prisoner. The buildings are permanent, substantial and fireproof, but the great majority of the prisoners will live in dormitories similar to those which are used for housing soldiers.

If the New York city authorities should decide that the cell-house plans of 1909 are satisfactory and within their means, they can build two cell houses on those plans: one for the distribution prison and one for the penitentiary.

Wooden office buildings can serve for several years to come, postponing the immediate erection of the central administration building, which will doubtless be the most expensive building on the Island. It is probable that the 1909 plans for hospital, shops and warehouse can be utilized.

I would earnestly recommend that the Commissioner, with other representatives of the City Government, visit some representative prisons, like the Westchester County Penitentiary at Eastview, the new Erie County Penitentiary near Buffalo, the District of Columbia Reformatory at Lorton, the Canadian prison at Guelph, Ontario, and the new Sing Sing Prison.

An inspection of these prisons will throw an illuminating light upon the problem of constructing a new institution on Riker's Island. In the light of the experience in the erection of the prisons above named I have no hesitation in saying that the plans of 1909 can be so modified as to save the city of New York from $500,000 to $1,000,000 without sacrificing anything essential in the buildings of the new penitentiary and the auxiliary departments above referred to.

If these suggestions were adopted, it would be possible to utilize this valuable property for the care of 5,000 to 6,000 prisoners instead of 350 drug addicts, and it would be possible to organize a productive industrial system, as contemplated by Chapter 601 of the laws of 1924, under which the prisoners could become, at least measurably, self-supporting.[1]

United Capacity.—The united capacity of the three departments on Riker's Island would be as follows:[2]

	Immediate capacity	Ultimate capacity
Distributing Prison	300 to 350	400 to 500
New Penitentiary	500 to 600	600 to 800
Prison for drug addicts	200 to 300	400 to 500
Total capacity	1,000 to 1,250	1,400 to 1,800

A Great Opportunity

Riker's Island, with a tract of 300 to 400 acres of land, containing only one small and inexpensive permanent building, offers a great opportunity to the city of New York to establish the most recent and the most practical institution for misdemeanant prisoners in the world. This undertaking is worthy of the most careful study in the light of recent institutions for misdemeanant prisoners erected by the cities of Cleveland, Kansas City, and Detroit, and the states of Massachusetts and Indiana and the District of Columbia. New York has the opportunity to avoid on the one hand the waste of money in expensive temporary buildings, and on the other hand the wasteful extravagance of some of the recent state prisons. This undertaking calls for intelligent and painstaking study. Other communities have spent millions of dollars in costly experiments, some of which succeeded while others have failed. New York may well profit by their experience.

For detailed information with reference to the prisons on Welfare, Hart's, and Riker's Islands, and the conditions on those islands, see my report filed November 20, 1924, which follows.

Yours respectfully,

HASTINGS H. HART.

[1] See pp. 34–36.

[2] These estimates are based on the expectation that the probation and parole systems will be perfected and expanded.

PART II
ORIGINAL REPORT OF NOVEMBER 20, 1924

REPORT OF A SPECIAL STUDY OF THE NEW YORK CITY PRISON SYSTEM

NEW YORK, NOVEMBER 20, 1924

HON. GEORGE W. WICKERSHAM,
New York City.

My dear Mr. Wickersham:

In accordance with your request of January 21, 1924, made in behalf of a group of organizations interested in the improvement of the prison system, I have made a study of the correctional institutions of the city of New York.

This study was made with special reference to the application of the Commissioner of Correction for an appropriation of $8,000,000 to be used for the "reorganization and reconstruction on modern lines and in suitable localities of the penal and correctional institutions of the city."

The city of New York, with its six million inhabitants, maintains a prison system of its own (not including prisoners committed from the city to the different state prisons) with more inmates than the entire prison population of any state except Alabama, Illinois, Massachusetts, Michigan, Missouri, New York, and Ohio.[1]

In this report I shall endeavor to view these institutions with a long forward look to the probable future needs of Greater New York and with reference to the relations of the institutions to each other and to the present and future distribution of the population of the city and its environs.

PRISONS ON WELFARE ISLAND

Welfare Island is used partly by the Department of Public Welfare, which maintains there hospitals and institutions for aged

---

[1] Report of the New York State Prison Commission for 1923; Report of the U. S. Bureau of the Census on Number of Prisoners in Penal Institutions, 1922 and 1917, published in 1923.

people. It is used partly by the Department of Correction, which maintains the following:

The New York County Penitentiary is located on Welfare Island. Although it is called a county penitentiary it has been for many years a city prison, maintained by the city of New York. It is one of the oldest institutions of the city. It contains 1,118 cells, of which 750 were built about 1830 and are now about 94 years old. These ancient cells are 3.5 x 7 x 7.5 feet, about the same size as the old cells at Sing Sing prison. There are about 368 cells, built in 1898, now 26 years old. These cells are one foot wider than the old cells, being 4.7 x 7.5 x 7 feet. There is no plumbing in any of the 1,118 cells; the ancient and abominable bucket system prevails throughout. There are three cell blocks, but they are so arranged as to make proper classification impossible. There are two large dormitories in the old industrial building which are not now needed and should not be used.

Its ancient buildings, its insanitary condition, its lack of provision for classification, its fire risks, and so on, have been described, periodically, for many years in the reports of successive commissioners of correction, grand juries, state commissioners of prisons and representatives of the Prison Association of New York.

The hospital at the penitentiary is inadequate and unsatisfactory because it does not provide for proper classification of patients and for segregation of contagious and infectious cases. It has been proposed to expend $65,000 in reconstructing the hospital to meet these needs.

I advise against the expenditure for this purpose. When the penitentiary is removed from Welfare Island, such an expenditure would be likely to become a total loss.

I recommend that the department make shift with the present inadequate hospital facilities until a permanent site for the penitentiary is selected and that the proposed hospital appropriation be expended on that site.

Employment of Prisoners.—There were 1,040 prisoners at the time of the visit, of whom about 750 had nominal employment. There is a garden of about seven acres which furnishes occupation for a small number of prisoners. The principal employment of the prisoners is the care of the roads, walks and grounds, the repair of the buildings of all kinds on the Island, the hauling of supplies from one part of the Island to another, the removal of garbage and rubbish, and the domestic work of the penitentiary.

The outside work furnishes employment for perhaps 250 prisoners, and the domestic work of the penitentiary employs from 500 to 600 men; but this work could be performed by half the number of men if they worked efficiently, as is illustrated by the fact that one form of employment is for several men to drag a large cart by hand.

It has come to be generally recognized that outdoor exercise and a reasonable amount of recreation are essential factors in any rational efforts to reform and redeem people of the classes that are found in these two correctional institutions; but the conditions on Welfare Island are such that there cannot be suitable enclosures for this purpose; neither is room available for establishing industrial plants nor for adequate gardens, poultry yards, and piggeries, to say nothing of a dairy.

Contraband.—A more serious difficulty is the fact that it is impossible, by any amount of vigilance, to prevent the introduction of drugs and other contraband material. It is proper and necessary that the hospitals and other institutions maintained by the Department of Public Welfare should be open to visitors a large part of each day. Such visitors come to Welfare Island in large numbers and pass up and down its public walks and roads. The Queensborough Bridge crosses the Island and is connected with it by elevators, both for foot passengers and vehicles. It is an easy matter for visitors to drop packages containing drugs and other contraband material, or for passengers on the street cars to throw such objects from the Bridge. The prisoners who do outside work in every part of the Island are constantly passing to and fro and have opportunity to gather up whatever may be left for them by passengers or visitors. If there were no other reason, this difficulty would be a sufficient cause for removing all prisoners from the Island. The majority of the patients in the Correction Hospital are drug addicts, and a large proportion of the prisoners in the penitentiary have the same habit. There is no hope of effecting a permanent cure of this tenacious habit unless its victims are prevented from obtaining the drugs which have been their curse.

The Penitentiary as a Clearing House.—The penitentiary was designated, three or four years ago, as a distributing prison. The theory was that all adult male prisoners belonging to the city should be first sent to the penitentiary, where they would receive physical, medical and mental examinations and then would be assigned to the branch penitentiary at Hart's Island, the hospital for drug addicts at Riker's Island, or the Reformatory for Young Men at New Hampton.

This clearing house idea has not yet been put into efficient operation. The penitentiary contains a mixed multitude of prisoners, some of whom have fixed sentences; some are subject to parole, some are drug addicts, some are crippled and worn-out old men. The penitentiary is kept pretty nearly full; it is so constructed as to make it very difficult to classify prisoners and there is unavoidably more or less contact and association between the newcomers and the old prisoners.

A large part of the prisoners remain in the penitentiary. Some are transferred to the branch penitentiary at Hart's Island, the hospital for drug addicts at Riker's Island, and the young men's reformatory at New Hampton,[1] where efforts are made for their reformation; but when the time comes for their parole or discharge they are returned to the penitentiary and are paroled or discharged therefrom. This method tends to dissipate the reformatory impression which they may have received and to weaken the influence of those who have worked for their improvement.

The idea of a central distribution prison—a clearing house, with observation wards, laboratories, medical, dental and mental clinics—is an admirable one; but it should be carried on in a comparatively small institution, entirely detached from the other city prisons, with buildings and equipment expressly designed for its work. This distributing prison need not have a capacity of more than 300 to 400 prisoners.

A New Distributing Prison

I would recommend that a suitable distributing prison, designed expressly for that purpose, and having a present capacity of not more than 300 to 400 prisoners, be erected, either on Riker's Island or on some other suitable and accessible site.

I would recommend further that when prisoners are transferred from the distributing prison their records and personal effects be

---

[1] I was informed that this system was about to be changed as far as the New Hampton Reformatory is concerned.

transferred with them, except an outline card record retained for reference; and that discharges and paroles be made directly from the different institutions in which they may have been detained, in order that parole officers may avail themselves of the prison records and the personal knowledge of the prisoners obtained by the prison officials who have had charge of them.

The present practice of re-transferring prisoners to the penitentiary before their discharge or parole involves much extra trouble and expense for which I can discover no compensating advantage.

The Correction Hospital is a combined hospital and prison for delinquent women, known as the Workhouse, with a normal capacity of about 150 hospital cases, chiefly drug addicts and venereal cases, and about 150 women prisoners sentenced by the Magistrates' Courts. It receives also a limited number of "self-committed" inmates who enter the hospital voluntarily for treatment.

This institution formerly received both male and female prisoners but has been used exclusively for women for several years past. The south wing of the institution was reconstructed several years ago for hospital purposes and was made fireproof. It has separate wards for medical, surgical, venereal and tubercular cases and for drug addicts, providing segregation for each class of patients. It has also a clinical department for medical, surgical and psychiatric examinations.

The prison department was built in the year 1852. It contains 104 cells or rooms, each about 13 x 10 x 18, with an outside window. There are also three dormitories which bring the total capacity of the prison department up to about 150 women.

While the wing used for the Correction Hospital is fairly well adapted to its present purpose, its location as a hospital for drug addicts is objectionable for the reasons already stated. The Department of Public Welfare can use this building to advantage for hospital purposes without any sacrifice of values, and a new site should be selected for the Correction Hospital.

The Women's Farm Colony at Greycourt.—The Correction Hospital need never be a large one, because the patients should be transferred to the Women's Farm at Greycourt as soon as their medical treatment is completed. In order to secure an open outdoor space it would probably be well to build a hospital with a good-sized central court, on a plan similar to that of the Women's Reformatory building at Marysville, Ohio. In March, 1924, the new City Reformatory for Women was opened and about 60 women were transferred from the Workhouse to Greycourt. It is expected that the Farm Colony will take the place of the prison department of the Correction Hospital, in which case the south wing of that institution should be torn down.

THE PRISONS ON WELFARE ISLAND SHOULD BE REMOVED

It is agreed by all of the authorities that the public interest calls for the abandonment of Welfare Island as a location for prisons.

By an act of the Legislature in 1895 it was provided that no more buildings should be built at Blackwell's Island and that, as soon as practicable, the buildings owned by said Department should be vacated and become the property of the Department of Public Charities. The purpose of this law was to force the removal of the correctional group of buildings now on Welfare Island to other islands or locations.

The New York City Charter of 1898, Chapter XIV, contains the following provision: "The Commissioner" [of Correction] "whenever in his judgment it is expedient and practicable . . . may cause to be removed to Riker's Island, and" [under certain prescribed conditions] "to Hart's Island, the inmates of the Workhouse and of the Penitentiary on Blackwell's" [Welfare] "Island."

In 1905 Commissioner Lantry, in a letter to Mayor McClellan, said:

"I fully agree with Mr. Homer Folks in the opinion that all future penal institutions under the jurisdiction of the Department of Correction should be erected on parts of Riker's Island."

In December, 1923, Hon. John S. Kennedy and Hon. Leon C. Weinstock, State Prison Commissioners, in their annual report, said:

"The penitentiary on Welfare Island must go. This wonderful island is needed for a playground for the people of New York."

On August 28, 1923, Commissioner Frederick A. Wallis recommended an appropriation for the building of a new penitentiary for the males on Riker's Island.

On August 26, 1924, Commissioner Bird S. Coler, of the Department of Public Welfare, addressed a letter to the secretary of the Grand Jury, in which he said:

"The Grand Jury . . . I understand, feel that it would be more advisable to remóve the City Prison from Welfare Island, rather than make expensive changes to the building. . . . Such a recommendation by the Grand Jury would . . . be a step forward.

"I have always been very strongly in favor of the making of Welfare Island a real center and home for the sick poor and aged destitute. . . . Every effort should be made to accomplish this at an early date.

"The removal of the Workhouse and the City Prison from Welfare Island would bring this about, as section 696 of the New York City Charter reads as follows. . . . 'Whenever any of the said buildings or grounds shall have been so transferred, the Commissioner of Correction shall have no further rights, duties or obligations in respect to such . . . buildings or grounds . . .'

"Hoping that the Grand Jury will lend its aid in making this possible, I remain, very truly yours,
"BIRD S. COLER, Commissioner."

In a statement to the Grand Jury in New York City, August 26, 1924, Commissioner Frederick A. Wallis, of the Department of Correction, said:

"Thirty-one years ago the necessity for building a new penitentiary in New York City was a paramount issue. If we had millions of money at our command, I don't think we should erect a penal institution on Welfare Island. . . .

"Probably the day will come . . . when all institutions of whatever character will be entirely removed and Welfare Island will be made a great park. . . .

"In 1908 . . . the Board of Estimate and Apportionment of the City of New York . . . authorized an issue of $200,000 for the . . . preparing of plans and specifications for a new penitentiary on Riker's Island. . . . We could erect on that island a great modern penitentiary."

HART'S ISLAND

The Branch Penitentiary, Hart's Island.—This prison is still called "The Reformatory Prison," although it has for several years been a branch of the Penitentiary. It receives male prisoners under penitentiary sentences, with a maximum of three years, and prisoners under workhouse sentences with a maximum of two years, both classes of prisoners being subject to parole. On the date of my visit, February 28, 1924, there were present 692 prisoners under penitentiary sentences, 157 under workhouse sentences, and two under reformatory sentences; total, 851.

The buildings are: administration building with four dormitories; hospital building with general and tuberculosis wards, capacity 40 patients, containing also dormitories for 74 officers; also one dormitory for prisoners (both these buildings are practically fireproof); a wood and brick dining hall containing three dormitories which are dangerous fire traps; a disciplinary building, power house, store house, stable and several residences.

The old men's department (not included above) consists of a group of antiquated wooden cottages built for veterans of the Civil War. These buildings are worn-out, rotten fire-traps in which the beds of the old men are crowded together. They contain no day rooms, and the poor old men lead a wretched existence in winter and in stormy weather. These inmates are worn-out old men, no longer capable of inflicting any serious damage upon society. Many of them are of the vagrant and intemperate classes. It is cruelty to turn such men loose on the streets of New York, and they sometimes secrete themselves when they are about to be discharged, because they prefer even this unhappy condition to vagrancy in the great city.

The Commissioner of Correction has urged legislation whereby men of this class can be transferred to the Almshouse instead of being committed and re-committed.

The Island contains about 77 acres of land, of which four acres belong to private parties, a fact which promotes escapes and the smuggling of drugs and other contraband materials. This land should be acquired by the city through condemnation proceedings in order to prevent these evils.

Hart's Island has been used for the past 50 years as a potter's field for the burial of the paupers. Already 241,000 burials have been made. During the past 10 years, 1914 to 1923, 58,273 bodies have been interred, a yearly average of 5,828. The bodies are buried in trenches 40 x 16 feet, three deep. The boxes containing the bodies are placed side by side in double rows, 25 in a row, so that 150 bodies of adults are interred in a space 40 x 16 feet, which is equal to 640 square feet. If we leave a space of only two feet between trenches, it will make 112 square feet additional or a total of 752 feet for each trench containing 150 bodies, which is five square feet for each body. The bodies of children, especially those of infants, occupy a much smaller space.

It is estimated that the 241,000 bodies already interred occupy about 15 acres. The burials at the present rate occupy probably about one-half acre yearly.

The city owns approximately 77 acres of ground on Hart's Island. Some of this ground is low and wet. Only a small portion is fit for gardening. I learned that about 16 acres are under cultivation, but this garden spot is gradually being absorbed for burial purposes, and if the present rate of burials continues it will probably be all used up in another 30 years.

Present Area of Hart's Island.—I estimate the present disposition of the land as follows:

For buildings and yard	18 acres
For old men's home	4 "
For burials	18 "
For exercise field	6 "
For gardens	15 "
Total	61 acres
Low ground not available	12 "
Owned by outside parties	4 "
Total area of Hart's Island at high tide	77 acres [a]

[a] Area at low tide, 113 acres.

There are a few old shop buildings on Hart's Island, but they are entirely inadequate for the employment of 700 prisoners. Immediate provision should be made for suitable shops with modern equipment to permit of the employment of the prisoners on the state's use plan. Such shops should have available from 2 to 6 acres of space, according to the kinds of industries to be pursued.

As already stated, the present capacity of the dormitories is 700 prisoners. The minimum amount of ground required for prison buildings, shops, storehouses, stables, and so forth for 700 prisoners, exclusive of gardens and recreation grounds, would be about 16 acres, or one acre for every 44 prisoners.

Under these circumstances it is evidently impracticable to provide additional prison facilities on Hart's Island unless the use of the Island as a burial place should be discontinued. An effort was made some years ago to substitute cremation for burial, which would be a most desirable change from every practical point of view. I understand that this plan was not actively opposed by the religious authorities of the various sects, but it was impossible to obtain unanimous agreement and the proposition was finally dropped.

If the bodies already interred on Hart's Island could be removed and cremated, the Island would furnish a good site for an industrial prison for not more than 700 prisoners. If the bodies are not removed and burials on the Island are continued, the number of prisoners should be reduced as the available land decreases; otherwise it will be impossible to provide the shop room, exercise grounds and gardens which are indispensable to a well-conducted modern prison and to the employment of the prisoners in such a way as to preserve their physical and moral health, to give them some degree of vocational training, and to permit them to earn at least a portion of the cost of their maintenance.

FUTURE LOCATION OF THE PENITENTIARY

I have recommended the removal of the penitentiary from Welfare Island and have shown that Hart's Island can not, under any circumstances, furnish an adequate site for more than 700 penitentiary prisoners—probably less. The question properly arises: Where then can provision be made for the remainder of the penitentiary population which at present amounts to more than 3,000 prisoners and is likely to increase.

Three possible solutions of this problem suggest themselves: first, the excellent site at Warwick, Orange County, 63 miles from New York City. This farm was purchased by the city a number of years ago, to be used as a site for a hospital for inebriates but was soon abandoned for that purpose. The farm consists of 650 acres of fairly good land with excellent building sites. It borders upon a beautiful lake about one and a half miles long and one mile wide. The lake is deep and furnishes an abundant supply of good water. It would be possible for the city to obtain control of the entire water-shed of this lake by purchasing the adjacent land, which could be had at a moderate cost by condemnation. A part of this land is suitable for dairy farming and a part is located on the mountain side and could be profitably forested by prison labor.

There is a fine old mansion which serves as an administration building, a well-furnished wooden dining room building, and a rather poorly constructed wooden dormitory with sleeping rooms for 60 prisoners. These buildings are within about an eighth of a mile of the institution's side track on the Lehigh and Hudson River Railway. This road extends southwest to Allentown, Pa., and northeast to Greycourt on the Erie Road, giving ready access to coal, iron and lumber, so that it would be possible to establish manufacturing industries advantageously.

The Warwick Farm is at present being operated as a dairy farm, being especially adapted to that purpose, and is furnishing milk and butter for the New York City Reformatory at New Hampton and the Women's Farm Colony at Greycourt. It would be entirely possible to produce butter and eggs for the public institutions in New York City.

Warwick has the advantage of being located in a region which is not occupied by suburban towns. The city already owns three farms in that vicinity and can escape the opposition which is necessarily encountered in locating such an institution in the vicinity of New York. The city is already committed to the policy of establishing institutions in that vicinity, and there would be advantages in grouping them there.

The suggestion has been made that the farms at Warwick and Greycourt should be sold. This would appear to be unwise unless the Department of Correction has in its possession suitable property to provide for prisoners of the penitentiary class for the next fifty years elsewhere. Prison buildings are of a permanent character and those which are now in use have some of them been occupied for nearly ninety years. It is no longer easy to find suitable sites for public institutions, and the difficulty will increase with the further development of the metropolitan area.

The objection to Warwick Farm as a site for the penitentiary is its distance from the city and the difficulty of reaching it, especially in winter, and the consequent inconvenience of the transportation of prisoners, visitors, public officials, and supplies.

PUTNAM COUNTY, ORANGE COUNTY OR LONG ISLAND

A second possibility of future provision for the penitentiary is to find a new site in some other locality than those now owned by the city and within a reasonable distance. The property of the city in Orange County is approximately 60 miles from the city, and it is undesirable to locate city institutions at a greater distance from the city because of the expense and inconvenience of transportation for public officers, inmates, visitors and supplies.

If city institutions are located within a distance of 60 miles from the Municipal Building, and beyond the present city limits, they must be located either on Long Island, in Westchester, Rockland, Putnam or Orange County. Westchester, Rockland and Putnam Counties are within the suburban area and efforts to locate large prisons within their boundaries would probably meet with bitter opposition and prohibitive cost. The state of New York has abandoned state institution sites at Yorktown Heights and Mohansic after expending about $1,000,000, because of intense opposition arising from the fact that these two sites were located on the Croton Watershed, and the taxpayers of Westchester County justly complain of the very large amount of property removed from the tax list because it is occupied by public or private institutions. This would leave available only Orange County, Putnam County and Long Island as possible locations for new city prisons, and it is probable that suitable sites could not be had on Long Island at reasonable prices without going to a distance approximately as far as the region of the three city farms in Orange County.

Riker's Island

A third possible site for the penitentiary, the best one proposed thus far, is Riker's Island. Riker's Island is situated in the East River, about half way between the mainland at 143d Street and Talman Island, at the entrance to Long Island Sound, about three-fourths of a mile from the mainland by ferry. Originally it was much smaller than at present, but it has been filled in to a present area of perhaps 400 acres, and I am informed that when the space already approved by the United States engineers is filled in there may be a total of approximately 750 acres.

Riker's Island, with an area of 400 acres or more and a prospect of 750, is used for only 350 drug addicts. The authorities object to bringing other classes of prisoners to the Island because of the necessity of isolating these people. The impracticability of this attitude is seen from the fact that Ward's Island, with an area of only 234 acres, has a population of 6,800 insane people, together with the necessary caretakers. If Riker's Island had as many in proportion it would contain a population of more than 15,000 people, with an ultimate capacity above 20,000. It is true that Ward's Island is wickedly overcrowded. It should not contain more than 1,500 people, or at most 2,000; but even at that rate Riker's Island could receive a population of 3,000 to 4,000 prisoners in the near future, with an ultimate population of 4,500 to 6,000. The Island is altogether too valuable and the need of the city for room for public institutions is too great to justify its use for so small a population as that of the male drug addicts of the hospital class.

Value of Riker's Island.—I have only an imperfect idea of the economic value of Riker's Island if it were devoted to manufacturing or residence purposes. I was informed that South Brothers' Island, lying between Riker's Island and Manhattan and containing about seven acres, held by private parties, is assessed at $40,000, which would be about $6,000 per acre (it was stated that the owners valued it at $1,000,000).

If South Brothers' Island is worth $6,000 per acre, the 500 acres of Riker's Island which is already available ought to be worth as much as $4,000 per acre, which would make a total of $2,000,000. If we reckon the rental value of this land at four per cent, it would amount to $80,000 a year, or about $230 ground rent for each of the 350 patients. The absurdity of this proposition is manifest. Riker's Island must ultimately serve the needs of a much greater population than it now contains.

Made Ground.—For many years the Island has been used as a dumping ground for ashes, street sweepings, boxes, barrels, bedsteads, mattresses, old iron and other waste material which are collected throughout the city and dumped at convenient points onto large barges which are towed to Riker's Island and unloaded by steam shovels which deposit the material on tram cars by which it is carried to dumping places.

Retaining walls are built to enclose low grounds or shallow water along the borders of the Island. The rubbish on hand is then dumped within these retaining walls and is gradually built up to a height of about 30 feet. Fires are kept constantly burning to consume partially the inflammable material and the new-made ground gradually settles as the materials decay. After several years the new ground is raked and harrowed, old iron, stone and so forth are disinterred and buried at greater depth, and gradually a soil is developed on which it is possible to raise vegetables. This soil is very porous and dries out rapidly so that it is necessary to plant early in the season. On the whole it is more productive than would be anticipated, but it is at best of poor quality for farming and gardening.

The Department of Street Cleaning has installed an incinerating plant at the foot of 56th Street in which the inflammable portion of the refuse material is consumed, greatly reducing the time required for the conversion of this material into cultivable soil. A second incinerating plant is to be installed later at or near East 134th Street.

I do not know whether, in the ultimate development of the city, Riker's Island will be needed for park purposes, but I shall assume for the purposes of this discussion that it will continue to be available for uses of the Department of Correction. On that assumption I offer the following suggestion as to its immediate and ultimate uses:

Present Use of Riker's Island.—The Island is used at present exclusively for hospital care and treatment of about 350 drug addicts who occupy wooden barracks of a temporary character. Similar buildings are used for officers' quarters, dining hall, kitchen, storerooms and other administrative buildings. There is only one building of a permanent character on the Island, a "disciplinary building," 35 x 110 feet, containing 40 large cells constructed in 1917; but this building is used only to a very limited extent. The buildings on Riker's Island are of so little value that they can be absolutely disregarded in considering the future use of the Island.

The availability of the Island for agricultural purposes would be greatly increased if a suitable top soil could be provided. I learned from the warden and from the mate on one of the steamers which plies between the Island and the mainland that there are large quantities of mud in portions of the East River, near to the shore. I made inquiries from the engineers of the United States Government and the city but was unable to get definite information. I would advise that a survey be made by competent engineers, that samples of the deposits around the Island be taken, and that tests be secured from competent soil experts of Cornell University.

If suitable material is available, it could probably be pumped from the river at a very moderate expense. This material would not only improve the quality of the soil but would probably hasten by two or three years the time when it would become available for cultivation.

Future Uses of Riker's Island.—Assuming that the Island is to be reserved for the next fifty years for the use of the Department of Correction, I recommend that plans be made immediately looking to the utilization of the entire Island to the extent of its reasonable capacity.

The Island Should not be Used Exclusively for Treatment of Drug Addicts.—It has been urged that the Island should be used exclusively for drug addicts because of the danger of the illicit introduction of such drugs if other classes of prisoners are kept on the Island. This objection can be met by taking proper measures for the segregation of this class of prisoners. As a matter of fact, a considerable number of free laborers are employed at the present time on the Island in dumping and grading the material brought from the city of New York. Apparently it has been possible to prevent any large amount of traffic in drugs through this channel and it is possible to prevent such traffic between different classes of prisoners. A tract of 15 or 20 acres, including the buildings now occupied by the hospital for drug addicts, can be set apart for that institution. This tract can be separated from the rest of the Island either by a wall or by two parallel barbed wire fences 10 feet high, separated by sufficient space to prevent the transmission of contraband materials.

The Penitentiary can be Transferred to Riker's Island.—Building plans should be adopted of a much simpler character than has prevailed in recent years. It has been demonstrated in different states that cell houses, shops, and other buildings can be erected entirely by prison labor, and that elaborate and palatial administration buildings are entirely unnecessary. The business of the penitentiary can be transacted in a one-story office building, warehouses, laundry and shops. A one-story auditorium can be built at the start, and suitable chapel buildings can be provided later.

Separate cells for individual prisoners are desirable for the greater part of the population, but suitable cell houses can be constructed at a much lower cost than is involved in some of the recent elaborate prisons. A considerable portion of the population can be suitably kept in dormitory buildings like those which are now being erected by the District of Columbia at Lorton, Virginia, at a cost of not more than one-third as much as the extravagant cell houses which have been built in different parts of the country.

It is a well-recognized principle of prison management that it is proper to employ prisoners upon work which is designed for the use of the state or the city. This principle applies to the erection of prison buildings, and I believe that there will be no controversy with reference to such use of prisoners if the plan is conceived and executed in good faith.

The New Distributing Prison Should Go to Riker's Island.— The New York County Penitentiary was designated, a number of years ago, as a distributing prison or clearing house. The theory was that all adult male prisoners belonging to the city should be first sent to the penitentiary, where they would receive physical, medical and mental examinations and then would be assigned to that one of the city prisons whose buildings, treatment, discipline and employment might be best adapted to his individual needs.

This clearing house idea has not yet been put into efficient operation. The penitentiary is used both for distribution and for permanent detention. It contains a mixed multitude of prisoners, some of whom have fixed sentences; some are subject to parole; some are drug addicts; some are crippled and worn-out old men. The penitentiary is kept pretty nearly full; it is so constructed as to make it very difficult to classify prisoners, and there is unavoidably more or less contact and association between the newcomers and the old prisoners.

A large part of the prisoners remain in the penitentiary. Some are transferred to the branch penitentiary at Hart's Island, the hospital for drug addicts at Riker's Island, and the young men's reformatory at New Hampton, where efforts are made for their treatment and reformation; but when the time comes for their parole or discharge they are returned to the penitentiary and are paroled or discharged therefrom. This method tends to dissipate the reformatory impression which they may have received and to weaken the influence of those who have worked for their improvement.

The idea of a central distribution prison—a clearing house with observation wards, laboratories, medical, dental and mental clinics—is an admirable one; but it should be carried on in a comparatively small institution, entirely detached from the other city prisons, with buildings and equipment expressly designed for its work. This distribution prison need not have a capacity of more than 300 prisoners.

Recommendations.—I would recommend that a suitable distributing prison, designed expressly for that purpose and having a present capacity of not more than 300 prisoners, be erected on Riker's Island.

While the distributing prison should be a small one, it should be most carefully designed by co-operation of the city architects, prison wardens, physicians, psychiatrists and other experts, in order to facilitate a complete and expert study of every incoming prisoner.

The distributing prison should be complete in itself and entirely separate and distinct from the other institutions on Riker's Island. It should have set apart to it a sufficient tract of land to provide ample room for additional buildings, exercise grounds and gardens. At least 75 acres should be allotted to the distributing prison.

I would recommend further that when prisoners are transferred from the distributing prison their records and personal effects be transferred with them, except an outline card record retained for reference; and that discharges and paroles be made directly from the different institutions in which they may have been detained in order that parole officers may avail themselves of the prison records and the personal knowledge of the prisoners obtained by the prison officials who have had charge of them.

The present practice of re-transferring prisoners to the penitentiary before their discharge or parole involves much extra trouble and expense for which I can discover no compensating advantage.

An Opportunity for Constructive Prison Labor.—At the present time the refuse material brought to Riker's Island in scows is unloaded and dumped by free labor. I recommend that as soon as the present contract expires, portable wooden barracks of a temporary character, similar to those now in use at Hart's Island, be built at a convenient distance from the dumping grounds, and that a sufficient number of penitentiary prisoners be placed on the Island to do this work. At the present time the city has at least 1,000 idle prisoners from whom a suitable force could readily be recruited.

This would be an excellent form of prison labor for a large part of the prisoners. It is unskilled labor, out of doors; it will furnish work the year round, which prisoners can perform as well as free laborers if they are properly fed and clothed in cold weather, and if a small cash compensation is allowed to stimulate their industry and interest.

If this material is handled by prison labor, it will be possible to detail a squad of low-grade men to pick out iron, stone and other indestructible materials, which will materially facilitate the subsequent clearing up of the soil. It will be possible also to use men of similar grade on the work of preparing the ground for cultivation, instead of the drug addicts who are for the most part inefficient.

If this recommendation is adopted, it will be necessary to build a high fence to separate the dumping grounds from those parts of the Island which will be devoted to permanent building purposes, but that is entirely feasible.

I am informed that an agreement has been reached between the Department of Street Cleaning and the Commissioner of Correction whereby the unloading of scows and distribution of material is to be done by penitentiary prisoners. Provision should be made for living accommodations on Riker's Island, separate and apart from the drug addicts. This provision can be made in temporary wooden buildings similar to those which are used for the drug addicts on Riker's Island.

Industrial Organization

If the penitentiary is removed to Riker's Island (or to Warwick) a practical industrial system, under a competent superintendent and with efficient guards competent to act as industrial foremen and with adequate pay, should be organized forthwith. Examples of successful organization of labor systems in short term prisons can be found at the Detroit House of Correction and the Allegheny County Workhouse at Pittsburgh, Pa.

At the present time the labor scheme of the prison system of the city of New York is hopelessly inefficient. It can never be really efficient until a rational plan is put in operation under competent leadership and with first-class equipment.

The labor system must be organized practically. A common laborer in the city of New York is expected to earn a living for himself, his wife, and two children; this notwithstanding loss of time for holidays, sickness, sprees, strikes, storms and lockouts. The prisoner loses no time for any of these causes except for occasional holidays. His food is prescribed by a dietitian; his teeth are cared for by a dentist; sick call is held every day, with free hospital treatment if needed. His employer pays no rent and figures no interest on his capital; yet in most of our prisons the convict does not earn the bare cost of his board and keep, to say nothing of any contribution for the support of his family. It has been proved in Minnesota, Michigan, Alabama, and other states that it is possible for the prisoner to earn his own way and to contribute something toward the support of his family; but this possibility cannot be realized as long as the prisoner continues to have no incentive to industry and interest in his work except the fear of punishment or the loss of good time.

This incentive is to be found: first, in the spirit and personality of the warden and his staff; second, in dealing with the prisoner as a human individual, and not simply as a part of a herd; and, third, in the payment of sufficient wages to form a normal factor in the selling price of the product.

The labor system must be organized with a view to vocational training. I have no sympathy with the very common teaching that it is wrong to take into account production as a legitimate factor in prison labor. I have already discussed this point. But I do agree heartily with the idea that we should endeavor to fit the prisoner to get a living for himself and his family after his release. This, however, cannot be done simply by giving him instruction in a trade for which he may or may not be fitted. The prisoner needs, first, a physical basis of good health; second, a mental basis of intelligence and understanding; third, a spiritual basis of courage, hope, conscience, and a sense of responsibility; fourth, friendly guidance and good will by the right kind of a parole officer after his release.

The prisoner needs what was pungently expressed by the discharged prisoner who called upon a New York pastor years ago seeking some encouragement. After a brief conversation the pastor said: "Now, my friend, what do you think you need most?" The prisoner eyed him shrewdly and then replied: "I think that I need a new heart—*and a little money.*" No matter how well disposed the discharged prisoner may be he will be reduced to a point of starvation within 24 hours unless he can find a job. When he seeks one he must either admit that he has been in prison, which is likely to prevent his employment, or he must invent a plausible lie—and one cannot establish character upon a lie. The Prison Association and the Salvation Army are helpful, but available jobs are often scarce.

FUTURE POPULATION OF CITY CORRECTIONAL INSTITUTIONS

I have made a study of the population of the correctional institutions maintained by the city, with a view to an estimate of the probable prison population in the future. I have compiled from the annual reports of the City Department of Correction: first, the number of prisoners committed and, second, the daily average census of prisoners for each fiscal year. I have computed the ratio of these prisoners to the estimated population of Greater New York from year to year, and have made a comparison of these ratios. This comparison is based upon the prison population of the year 1915, when the numbers reached the highest peak ever recorded. These facts are displayed in Tables I and II which follow:

TABLE I.—PRISONS OF NEW YORK CITY.[1] PRISONERS RECEIVED
(Compiled from Annual Reports of Department of Correction)

Reports, of N. Y. Department of Correction		Prisoners received from courts	Per cent of number in 1915	Estimated population of Greater New York	Prisoners for each 100,00 of population	Comparative ratios based on 1915
Year	Page					
1915	40	86,625	100%	5,225,000	1,658	100
1916	92	64,383	74	5,312,000	1,210	73
1917	26	57,146	66	5,400,000	1,059	64
1918	45	49,611	57	5,488,000	904	55
1919	49	45,562	53	5,576,000	817	49
1920	129	40,832	47	5,664,000	721	45
1921	129	46,833	54	5,752,000	816	49
1922	50	60,472	70	5,847,000	1,036	62
1923	—[2]	50,706	59	5,947,000	852	51

[1] Not including inmates of police stations or the five county jails of greater New York.
[2] Figures furnished in advance of publication.

The facts recorded in Table I are graphically displayed in Diagram A.

Diagram A

PRISONS OF NEW YORK CITY
PRISONERS RECEIVED FROM COURTS, 1915 TO 1923

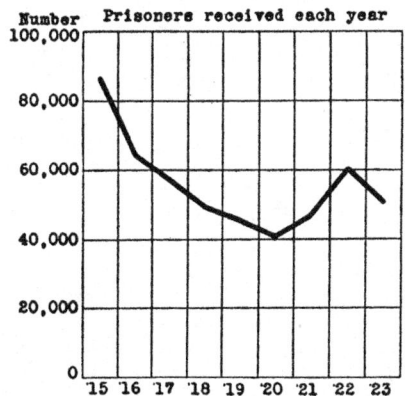

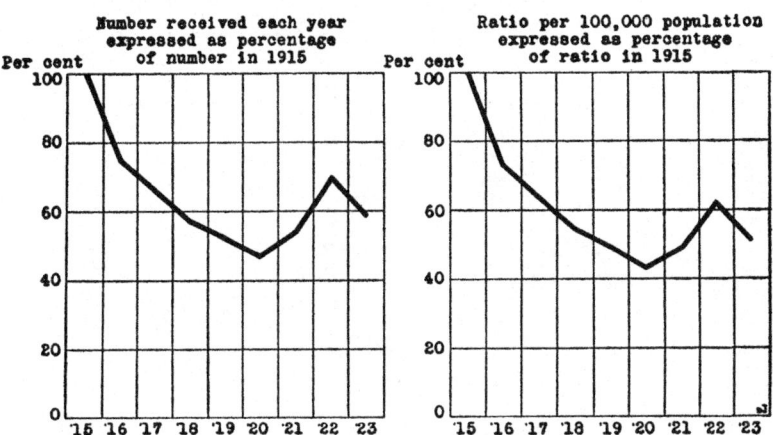

For supporting data see Table I

The figures in Table I are interesting, in view of the popular idea as to the great increase of the criminal population. While the number of prisoners received from the courts in 1922 showed a marked increase over the minimum which was reached in 1920, it was still only 70 per cent of the maximum reached in 1915. If the comparison is made with the population of Greater New York, as estimated by the United States Census Bureau, it appears that the ratio of prisoners to the population, as compared with 1915, was 45 per cent in 1920, 62 per cent in 1922, and only 51 per cent in 1923. The figures for 1924, not yet published, will probably show some increase but will still be below those of 1915.

It will be observed that the commitments fell off during the war to 1,166 in 1918, and reached their peak with 2,865 commitments in 1920, this number being almost identical with that of the year 1923.

TABLE II.—PRISONS OF NEW YORK CITY—AVERAGE NUMBER OF PRISONERS
(Compiled from Annual Reports of Department of Correction)

Reports of N. Y. Department of Correction, Year	Average Number of Prisoners	Per Cent of Number in 1915	Estimated Population of Greater New York	Prisoners for each 100,000 of Population	Comparative Ratios Based on 1915
1915	6,416	100	5,225,000	123	100
1916	5,079	79	5,312,000	96	78
1917	5,176	81	5,400,000	96	78
1918	4,202	65	5,488,000	77	62
1919	3,567	56	5,576,000	64	52
1920	2,997	47	5,664,000	53	43
1921	3,732	58	5,752,000	65	53
1922	4,219	66	5,840,000	72	58
1923	3,820	60	5,928,000	64	52

In Tables I and II the same general trend is seen, both as to the prisoners received and the average number. Referring to the right hand column of Table II, it will be seen that comparative ratio of prisoners to the city population decreased each year from 100 per cent in 1915 to 43 per cent in 1920; it increased to 58 per cent in 1922, but dropped back to 52 per cent in 1923.

Diagram B

PRISONS OF NEW YORK CITY
DAILY AVERAGE NUMBER OF PRISONERS, 1918 TO 1923

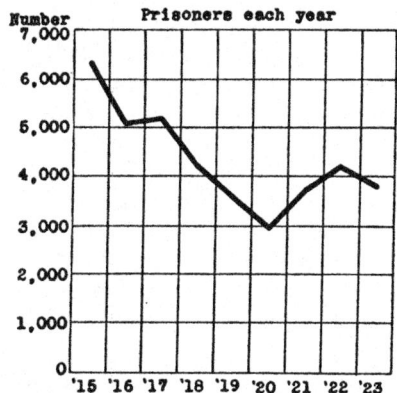

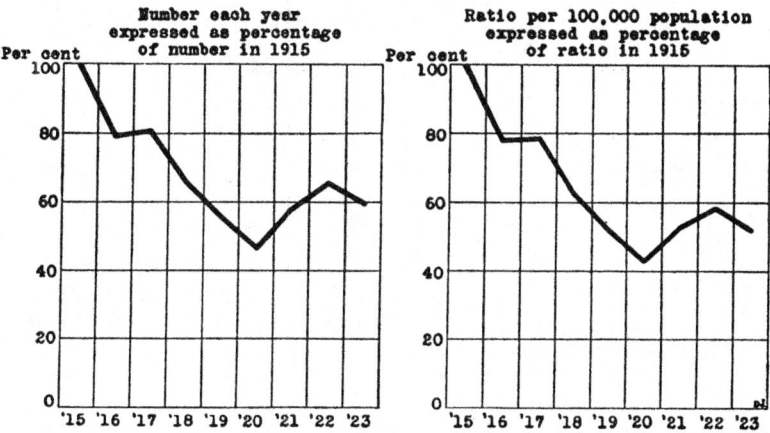

For supporting data see Table II

The facts displayed in Table II are graphically shown in Diagram B.

The gratifying reduction here shown in the population of the prisons of New York City is due to a variety of causes: first, the healthy reaction from war conditions; second, the great improvement in labor conditions; third, prohibition; fourth, the probation system. The diminution of the city prison population has been much greater than that of the state prisons and adult reformatories of New York, whose population is not greatly affected either by the probation system or by prohibition. Their population decreased from a relative ratio of 100 in 1915 to 64 in 1920, and then increased to 81 in 1922, as against 62 in the city prisons.

TABLE III.—PRISONS OF NEW YORK CITY—TOTAL NUMBER IN CUSTODY, SEPTEMBER 30
(Compiled from Annual Reports of Department of Correction)

	1915	1916	1917	1918	1919	1920	1921	1922	1923
City Prisons, Manhattan, Brooklyn and Queens	1,206	964	1,050	1,155	949	694	877	859	802
Eight District Prisons	250	257	233	166	190	148	113	112	141
Penitentiary and Workhouse	3,189	2,766	2,956	2,246	1,761	1,485	1,899	2,763	2,320
City Reformatory	455	360	449	497	458	395	304	355	212
Women's Hospital and Workhouse	617	694	594	418	342	146	221	341	318
Totals[1]	5,717	5,041	5,282	4,482	3,700	2,868	3,414	4,410	3,793
Prisoners for each 100,000 population[1]	109	95	98	82	66	51	59	75	64
Comparative ratios based on 1915[1]	100	87	90	75	61	47	54	69	59

[1] These figures differ from those of Table II because Table II shows the average number of prisoners for the year and Table III shows the number at the end of the year.

It is impossible at this time to predict what will be the prison population of the city ten years or twenty years from now. If probation is further expanded, as in Massachusetts; if the parole system is made much more efficient by improving the number and quality of parole officers, and if prohibition is reasonably enforced, there will probably be comparatively little increase in the prison population of the city; but if probation, parole and prohibition are inefficient, a large increase of the prison population may be expected.

It will be observed that in all of these institutions we have a maximum in 1915 and a minimum in 1920, then an increase to 1922 with a drop in 1923.

Table IV compares the average number of prisoners in the New York City prisons with their normal capacity. Every prison should have, at all times, some surplus room in order to be ready for incoming prisoners and also to give a margin for classification; but, notwithstanding the decrease in the number of prisoners the prisons of the city, with a normal capacity of 4,033, contained 3,743 prisoners at the close of the fiscal year 1923. Some of them had surplus cells, while others, as we have seen, were greatly overcrowded.

TABLE IV.—PRISONS OF NEW YORK CITY—POPULATION COMPARED WITH CAPACITY

(Compiled from Annual Reports of Department of Correction)

	Largest Number in 8 years	Average Number 8 years	Normal Capacity	Average Number in 1923
Manhattan City Prison[1]	648[2]	493	390	368
Brooklyn City Prison	304	267	416	266
Queens City Prison	202	91	209	85
Totals, City Prisons	1,154	851	1,015	719
Eight District Prisons	257	180	161	108
Penitentiary and Workhouse	3,189	2,376	2,179	2,320
Men's Reformatory	497	387	318	212
Totals, Prisons for Men	5,097	3,794	3,673	3,359
Women's Hospital and Workhouse	694	410	300	318
Women's Farm Colony[3]	..	..	60	66[3]
Grand Totals[4]	5,791	4,204	4,033	3,743

[1] Males only.
[2] Before the war sometimes as many as 900.
[3] Opened 1924, population for that year.
[4] Not including prisoners in police stations and the five county jails of Greater New York.

The table shows that the Manhattan City Prison, The Tombs, with a normal capacity of 390, had an average of 493 for a period of eight years, the number at the close of one year being 648 (before the war the number ran as high as 900). On the other hand, the city prisons of Brooklyn and Queens have seldom if ever been full to their normal capacity. The eight district prisons of the city of New York, with a normal capacity of 161, show an average for eight years of 180 and have sometimes run 100 above their capacity.

The New York County Penitentiary, with its branches on Hart's Island and Riker's Island, having a combined capacity of 2,178, contained in 1915, 3,189 prisoners (1,000 above capacity) and averaged for eight years 200 more than the normal capacity. The average number in 1923 was 141 above capacity.

The City Reformatory of New Hampton is only half completed. During the past eight years its average population has been 387, with a normal capacity of 318. At the close of 1918 the number was 497, which was 179 in excess of its capacity.

These conditions have resulted in overcrowding in the prisons of the city, which has produced much suffering and demoralization among the prisoners, a condition which is illustrated at the present time in the dormitories of the feeble old men at Hart's Island, who are crowded together in wretched wooden shacks, without living rooms, with a dangerous fire risk under inhuman conditions.

Treatment of Drug Addicts

An Irrational System.—The system of dealing with drug addicts in the past, both male and female, has been irrational and unscientific. Some of the patients have been committed on penitentiary sentences with a maximum of three years; some on workhouse sentences with a maximum sentence of two years, subject to parole in either case; many have been committed on a definite sentence of 100 days, under which they could not be paroled but must be discharged at the expiration of the time for which they were sentenced; some have been "self-committed," being received at their own request for treatment. Under the first of these plans the prisoner might be dismissed before the expiration of the sentence, under the guardianship and advice of a parole officer and subject to return to prison if he failed to comply with the conditions of his parole. Under the second system the prisoner might be released at the expiration of 100 days, whether he was regarded as "cured" or not. He went out penniless and friendless except for the interest of his former associates, who stood ready to supply him with "dope" immediately upon his discharge. The records at Riker's Island and the Women's Correction Hospital show that many drug addicts have been recommitted six, eight or ten times and some as many as twelve, fourteen or fifteen times. It costs the city of New York about $3 a day for the care and treatment of each one of these patients. If a prisoner is committed fifteen times, the city will have expended $4,500 in an utterly vain endeavor which was bound to fail from the start.

Patients of the third class, those who are self-committed, have been accustomed to think themselves superior to their fellow patients; they have been impudent and lawless, stirring up mischief and refusing to work. They have considered that they were entitled to leave the institution at their own pleasure.

Earnest efforts are being made by the Commissioner of Correction and the Superintendent of the Municipal Farm at Riker's Island to remedy these conditions, but a complete reorganization of the system is needed. The present futile plan should be abandoned.

The treatment of drug addicts is partly a hospital problem and partly a prison problem. The drug addict needs first a course of hospital treatment to establish the physical foundation which is the indispensable basis for his restoration to a normal condition. This course of treatment may require from four to six weeks, according to the condition of the patient when received. He needs, second, a course of reformatory treatment, with occupational therapy, which would include actual constructive work. This reformatory treatment should continue for as long a period as necessary, varying with the condition and needs of the individual and increasing in length with each successive recommitment. It should continue not less than three months and in confirmed cases might reach a maximum of three years.

A Rational Plan.—A law should be passed providing that all drug addicts shall be received by a court commitment and that they shall be committed just as insane patients are committed to a hospital—"*until cured.*" Provision should be made by law for a trial to determine the question whether the individual is a habitual user of a narcotic drug. When an individual is convicted of any crime, if at any time there is reason to believe that he is a drug addict, the superintendent, warden or other officer in charge of him should be required to file a petition for a trial to determine this question, and the law should be so framed that such criminals shall be placed under treatment and shall not be discharged from custody before they are deemed to be cured.

All drug addicts should be released on parole subject to close friendly supervision by probation officers of special adaptability and faithfulness. The system should be such that those paroled who go back to the use of drugs shall be promptly discovered and returned immediately for further treatment. The maximum term should not be less than three years and might well be even five years.

The law should be framed also to make reasonable and wholesome labor a part of the treatment of such individuals and to give the superintendent full authority to require such labor.

Such legislation with reference to the treatment and control of drug addicts is necessary, both for the protection of society, because the habit unquestionably promotes criminality, and also for the protection of the victim, who can be saved only by a protracted and vigorous course of treatment. It is no kindness to these individuals to leave them to perish through their own weakness or to suffer tortures through repeated courses of futile treatment. Our present practice is like the familiar story of the Dutchman and the dog's tail:

A friend inquired: "Hans, what makes your little dog look so sick?" "Why, somebody says, 'Your dog would look better if his tail was cut off.' I thought it would hurt the poor little dog too much if I cut off his tail all at once; so I cut off an inch every week."

A New Hospital for Drug Addicts.—I would recommend that the present temporary shacks now used as a hospital for drug addicts on Riker's Island be replaced by a more stable and permanent plant having a capacity of not more than 300 patients, but planned with reference to subsequent enlargement. Some difficulty will probably be experienced in getting a stable foundation for such buildings, but it can doubtless be overcome by the use of concrete piles.

A Reformatory for Drug Addicts.—I would recommend that a third independent plant be provided on Riker's Island with a capacity of 500 to 600 prisoners, subject to subsequent enlargement. This plant should be a reformatory prison to which should be transferred all drug addicts after the completion of their course of hospital treatment, which will usually require not more than thirty days. To this reformatory for drug addicts should be transferred all sentenced prisoners who are found to be addicted to the use of drugs. Such prisoners are now scattered through the six prisons where sentenced prisoners are kept; namely, The Manhattan City Prison (the Tombs); the Brooklyn City Prison (Raymond Street Jail); The New York County Penitentiary on Blackwell's Island; the branch penitentiary on Hart's Island; the City Reformatory at New Hampton; and the New Hampton Honor Camp at Warwick. These prisoners have spread the dire infection of drug addiction by smuggling in drugs and initiating other prisoners in their use.

Superintendent Schleth estimates that at the present time there are from 800 to 1,000 drug addicts in the various city prisons and he believes that if all of them were concentrated in a single institution it would contribute materially to check the spread of the drug habit, and would make it possible to establish a practical and effective plan for treating drug addicts.

Table V shows the number of commitments of drug addicts to the men's hospital at Riker's Island and the Women's Correction Hospital at Welfare Island from 1917 to 1923.

TABLE V.—CITY PRISONS OF NEW YORK—COMMITMENTS OF DRUG ADDICTS

Year	Men at Riker's Island	Women in Correction Hospital	Total
1917	1,624	231	1,855
1918	1,013	153	1,166
1919	1,498	190	1,688
1920	1,545	440	1,995
1921	1,984	152	2,136[1]
1922	2,194	242	2,436
1923	2,349	314	2,663

[1] During a period of three months the law for committing drug addicts was not in force.

The reformatory for drug addicts should be an industrial prison. Intensive farming should be carried on, and the institution should produce vegetables for the use of the various city institutions of the Department of Correction and the Department of Public Welfare. Farming, however, can employ only a fraction of the prisoners for a part of the year. It will be necessary, therefore, to establish a manufacturing industry on the public use system. This is entirely feasible. It is commonly supposed that drug addicts cannot do efficient work; but any one can disabuse himself of this notion by observing the work of the women drug addicts at the Correction Hospital on Welfare Island in the laundry. These women, after completing their course of medical treatment, work cheerfully and efficiently; but like the men from Riker's Island, most of them go to pieces immediately after their release because they are discharged without money, suitable clothing or helpful friends.

Table VI shows the average number of drug addicts on Riker's Island for each year from 1918 to 1922.

TABLE VI.—DRUG ADDICTS AT RIKER'S ISLAND

Year	Yearly Average
1918	394
1919	286
1920	303
1921	372
1922	401
1923	350

If the plan is adopted of transferring the drug addicts from the hospital department after medical treatment of perhaps 60 days, a hospital provision for 300 to 400 patients will probably be sufficient for a number of years to come.

Conclusion

The foregoing report contains little that is new. I have verified, by my own observation, facts which have been set forth over a period of many years in the reports of the Department of Correction of the city of New York, the New York State Prison Commission, the Prison Association of New York and other authorities, and have presented them in condensed form and logical order.

I sympathize heartily with the spirit and purpose of the Commissioner of Correction, and I believe that he is on the right track. It appears to me, however, that the questions which I have raised with reference to the permanent location of the Penitentiary, the

Distribution Prison and the hospitals for drug addicts, together with the question as to the general sites of future buildings and construction, should be definitely settled before embarking upon a comprehensive prison program.

I would recommend that the three organizations which have asked for this report, the Prison Association of New York, the National Committee on Prisons and Prison Labor, and the New York State Charities Aid Association, tender their assistance and co-operation to the city authorities in reaching a satisfactory solution of these questions.

I desire to express my appreciation of the courtesies and assistance which have been freely given to me in this inquiry by Commissioner Frederick Wallis and Major S. W. Brewster of the Department of Correction, and by the wardens and physicians of the several prisons. I am impressed by their manifest desire to serve the interests of the city and of the delinquent and diseased people who are committed to their care.

Hoping that this report may contribute in some degree to the solution of the complex and difficult prison problem which confronts the city of Greater New York, I am,

Yours respectfully,

HASTINGS H. HART.

To renew the charge, book must be brought to the desk.

TWO WEEK BOOK
DO NOT RETURN BOOKS ON SUNDAY

DATE DUE

Form 7079 6-52 30M S

BOUND

JAN 19 1936

UNIV OF MICH
LIBRARY

Printed in Dunstable, United Kingdom